Play at First Sight

The Ultimate Musician's Guide to Better Sight-Reading

Lalo Davila

© 2006 Alfred Publishing Co., Inc.
16320 Roscoe Blvd., Suite 100 • P.O. Box 10003
Van Nuys, CA 91410-0003

ISBN: 0-7390-4489-3
ISBN-13: 978-0-7390-4489-6

Alfred

Table of Contents

Introduction 3

Foreword 4

Acknowledgements 5

About the Author... 5

The Metronome... 6

Variations on the Metronome 6

How the Book Works... 7

Recognizing Groups of 16th Notes 8

16th-Note Timing and Reading Exercises in 4/4 9

Long and Short Notes 11

Tied Notes.. 12

Triplet Exercises in 4/4 13

Combining Triplets with Rests (Groups of Two) 14

The Quarter-Note Triplet... 16

Understanding Quarter-Note Triplets................................... 17

Quarter-Note Triplets with Rests (Beats 1 and 2; 2 and 3) 18

Quarter-Note Triplets with Eighth-Note Patterns (Beats 2 and 3; 3 and 4) 19

Quarter-Note Triplets with Eighth-Note Patterns (Beats 1 and 2) 20

Quarter-Note Triplets with Rests (Beats 3 and 4).................... 21

Quarter-Note Triplets with Half Notes and Rests 21

Quarter-Note Triplets with Eighth-Note Patterns (Beats 1 & 2; 3 & 4) 22

16th-Note Triplets.. 23

Sextuplet Exercises 24

Two-Beat Sextuplet Exercises... 25

Three-Beat Sextuplet Exercises... 26

Beat Cells 27

Jump-Around Measure Exercises.. 41

Two Measure Jump-Around Exercises (Nos. 1–4)................... 42

Three Measure Jump-Around Exercises (Nos. 1–4) 44

Four Measure Jump-Around Exercises (Nos. 1–4)................... 46

Five Measure Jump-Around Exercises (Nos. 1–4)................... 48

Six Measure Jump-Around Exercises (Nos. 1–4) 52

Seven Measure Jump-Around Exercises (Nos. 1–4) 56

Eight Measure Jump-Around Exercises (Nos. 1–4) 60

Bar None 64

Bar None (Nos. 1–5)..65–69

The Process for Performing the 42 Studies 70

Studies 1–42 71–112

Closing Remarks 113

Appendix 114

How to Apply the 42 Studies to Each Instrument 116

Articulation Suggestions for Wind Instruments...................... 118

Articulation Suggestions for Vocalists 119

CD Styles and Track Listing... 120

Introduction

Do you ever wonder why drummers and percussionists can read rhythms so well? Let me try and explain. Do you remember your first day in beginning band, or your first private lesson? As a non-drummer, you were basically taught how to put your instrument together, correct posture, embouchure, tone production, and even your very first note. As drummers/percussionists, we were taught the same thing, except on different instruments. All of us were taught the whole note and whole rest as our first rhythms. Although this is considered to be a good starting point, there was one big difference between what the percussionists and non-percussionists were taught. As a non-percussionist, you played or sang a note that contained sound being produced for four counts with a release on beat five. As a percussionist, depending on which instrument we were playing, we basically struck the drum once and counted through the duration of the whole note. If you think about it, there was not a sustained sound.

Therefore, in an effort to create a sustained-type of sound, percussionists were given extra notes of different duration to perform while wind players and vocalists played only a whole note. More than likely, the notes a percussionist would play to fill the space under a sustained sound would consist of quarter notes, eighth notes, or even 16th notes. Variations of all the above were used, as well, to create a sustained sound. So you see, even at an early age, percussionists were reading more complicated rhythms at a faster pace than non-percussionists. They were able to start recognizing rhythmic figures at sight and produce them without hesitation. As percussionists progressed through their studies, the use of rolls and other types of embellishments became a part of their "rhythm dictionary."

I call it a "rhythm dictionary" because percussionists have read various types of rhythmic figures that, by repetition, have become easy to recognize and perform. In most cases, wind players and vocalists have become better at performing melodies than percussionists who have only played membrane instruments (excluding those who were trained on keyboard instruments). It is my hope that this book will help strengthen your ability to recognize rhythms quickly and perform them as confidently as possible. The more you practice the exercises and variation possibilities on each page, the more at ease you will become at sight-reading rhythms.

Foreword

There are 42 studies in the back of this book. Each study has 10 staves that consist of four bars per stave. When performed with repeats, there are 80 measures per study. There are several tracks on the enclosed CD that include a variety of genres. All of the studies can be played with any of the tracks, except for those tracks that specifically correspond to the odd-meter studies.

Each line of the 42 studies consists of rhythms written above and below a single-line staff. The purpose is to force the performer to concentrate on sight-reading rhythms, and not just the melody and/or notes. When applying notes to the studies, the rhythms below the line should be played using the tonic/root of the chord in the key of the CD track. For the rhythms above the line, play the dominant/fifth of the chord.

Articulations and dynamics have been purposely left out so as to allow for the full concentration of rhythms first. Once you feel comfortable with the rhythms, you can go back and add dynamics and articulations.

There are numerous variations to learning how to sight-read. I will assure you that my method is neither exceptionally creative or innovative, but it is has worked for my students throughout my playing and teaching career. The key to improving sight-reading skills is to play **without stopping**. Stopping is a common mistake which results in getting lost in the music (making it difficult to figure out where you are). I encourage students to keep playing (no matter what), even if it means making up rhythms until you figure out where you are.

Acknowledgements

Although I have spent most of my career teaching and performing percussion, I have also spent many years working with non-percussionists. My experiences have included high school, junior high and elementary band. I have also spent the last few years teaching salsa music at the university level. I am thankful for all these opportunities.

I would like to thank all of my friends and colleagues for their encouragement: To Julie, my wife and friend, for her trust and for always believing in me; To my beautiful daughters, Danielle and Marisa, for filling me with joy and love; To my brothers and sisters, Mamie, Ralph, Hector, Chela and Ruben, for always being there when I needed them and for their never-ending love and prayers; To my mom and dad, who live in my heart, for teaching me to believe in myself; To all my students, past, present and future, who are now performers and educators, for providing me with great teaching and learning experiences; To all of my former teachers whose endless dedication to education has served as a model for my teaching and performance career. I would also like to the thank the following musicians who played on the accompanying CD: Stephen Kummer (piano), Jeff E. Cox (bass), Scott Gerow (guitar) and Johnny Rabb (drums); And, to God, for having blessed me with a beautiful life and a great career in music.

About the Author

Lalo Davila is currently Professor of Music and Director of Percussion Studies at Middle Tennessee State University. He received his Bachelor of Music degree from Corpus Christi State University and a Master of Music degree from the University of North Texas. Originally from Corpus Christi, Texas, Lalo has extensive experience both as an educator, composer, author, and performer. In addition, Mr. Davila was the recipient of Nashville's Top Five 1998 Percussionist of the Year Award. He spent three years (1984–1986) performing with and instructing the University of North Texas Percussive Arts Society Championship Drum Line, and has served as an instructor for the Phantom Regiment and the Star of Indiana Drum and Bugle Corps. Lalo has toured with many artists including the Take 6 summer 1996 tour of Japan. Other performances include the Corpus Christi Symphony Orchestra, the Nashville Symphony, the Nashville Jazz Orchestra, the Nashville Chamber Orchestra, the Nashville Chamber Chorus, the Nashville Ballet, Six Pence and None The Richer, Clay Walker, Vickie Carr, and Sherry Lewis to name a few. Mr. Davila has recently performed percussion and lead vocals for the American Bible Society CD project and can also be heard on Kirk Whalum's Grammy-nominated CD. Currently, Lalo performs with several Latin groups including "Orkesta Eme Pe."

Known as an outstanding clinician and adjudicator, Lalo has conducted clinics throughout the United States, Australia, Paris, Mexico, Cuba and Japan. Lalo is the author of *Contemporary Rudimental Studies and Solos*. Lalo is an active clinician/ performer for the Pearl Corporation, Row-Loff Productions, Avedis Zildjian Co., Innovative Percussion, and EVANS Drumheads.

The Metronome

- Practice with a metronome that has subdivision capabilities, or buy a drum machine and use it as a metronome.

- Start at a slow or moderate tempo, and increase the tempo as needed.

- While reading the rhythms, ALWAYS LOOK AHEAD and DO NOT STOP!

- Keep a log of your progress for each exercise and study.

- Play the exercises, along with the tracks, on the enclosed CD. Each track represents various tempos and styles.

Variations on the Metronome

- Start with the metronome sounding on all four beats.

- Switch the metronome to sound on 2 and 4 only (i.e., jazz style, etc.).

- Switch the metronome to sound on 1 and 3.

- Change the strong beat (high pitch) of the metronome to beat 2.

- Change the strong beat of the metronome to beat 3.

- Change the strong beat of the metronome to beat 4.

- Switch the metronome to eighth-note subdivisions.

- Take out the downbeats of the eighth note and play to the upbeats.

- Program the metronome so it only sounds on beat 1 of each measure, **and nothing else**.

- Use the above setting and think of it as beat 2.

- Use the above setting and think of it as beat 3.

- Use the above setting and think of it as beat 4.

- Using the same isolated beat, think of it as the upbeat of 1 and play the exercises/studies. Do the same for the upbeat of 2, 3 and 4.

- Program the metronome so it only sounds on beat 1 of every other measure.

These suggestions regarding the use of the metronome are few, but I am sure they will keep you busy and perhaps encourage you to try your own variations.

How the Book Works

The first section of the book contains several exercises to help the performer successfully execute rhythms commonly found in various musical settings. These exercises include a break down of eighth notes, 16th notes, triplets, sextuplets, and their respective rests. Variations of each exercise are used to help keep each fresh and interesting for the performer. The singing of each exercise and study is recommended throughout the book, as well as the use of a metronome.

The middle part of the book introduces "beat cells" and "jump-around measures," which are used to help train performers to look ahead when reading music. This approach is a lot of fun and never gets boring. The variations are limitless. There are also exercises that will help improve the reading of repeat signs, codas, dal segnos, and so on.

The last part of the book contains 42 individual studies. The studies are to be played along with the enclosed CD. All of these studies consist of rhythms that are written above and below a single-line staff. The purpose is to force the student to concentrate specifically on rhythmic execution, rather than on melodic structure. Numerous variations to the 42 studies are located in the back of the book. Applications for individual instrument groups can also be found at the back of the book.

The rhythms in the 42 studies have been written with articulations commonly found in various musical genres such as salsa, merengue, pop, soul, fusion, funk, and so on. The tracks on the enclosed CD represent examples of these same genres. So, not only are you working on your rhythm-reading chops, but you're also performing rhythms with proper stylistic interpretations. I hope you enjoy the book and that it will help you become a better sight-reader of rhythms. Good luck and remember to have fun!

About the CD

The enclosed play-along CD will be an invaluable tool in helping you to become a better sight-reader. Incorporating a variety of musical styles, each track begins with a two-measure introduction and continues for 80 measures (with a release on the downbeat of measure 81). The tonic can be used as the last note on the downbeat of measure 81 for each study.

Recognizing Groups of 16th Notes

The exercises below will help you recognize groups of 16th notes before you play them. Line A contains four groups of 16th notes. Line B contains eight groups of eight 16th notes. Line C contains twelve groups of 16th notes. And, line D contains an entire measure of 16th notes. Play the reference measure in between lines A, B, C and D. When playing the reference measure, look ahead to the next line to be performed. This will help you recognize rhythms before you play them. When comfortable, change the reference measure from quarter notes to eighth notes.

Reference Measure:

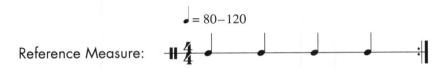

Line A:

Line B:

Line C:

Line D:

16-Note Timing and Reading Exercises in 4/4

Below are exercises that contain 16th notes, quarter notes and 16th-note rests. The first example is a reference line to show you that the exercises that follow are based on this four-measure figure. Be sure to memorize the rhythm patterns you think are giving you problems. This will make sight-reading easier down the road. Notice how the 16th-note figure is moved over by a beat from one measure to another.

Reference Line: ♩ = 80–120

8. 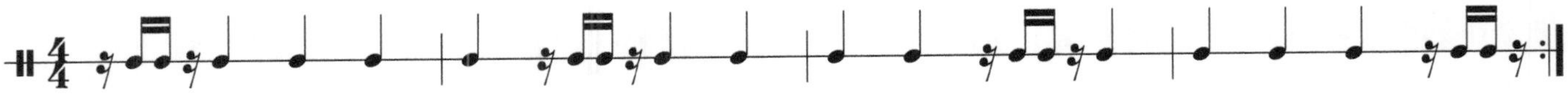

9. 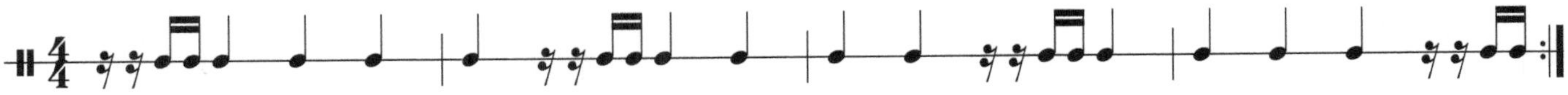

10. 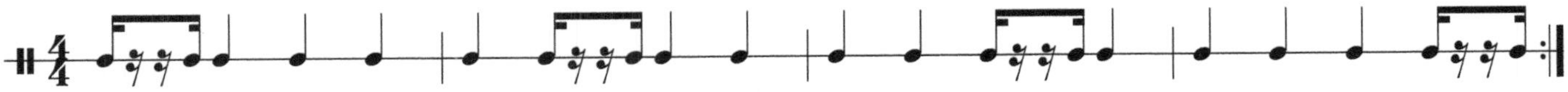

11. 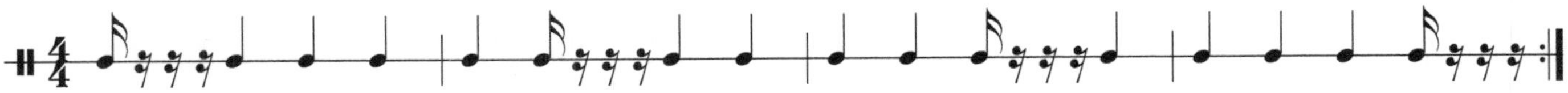

12. 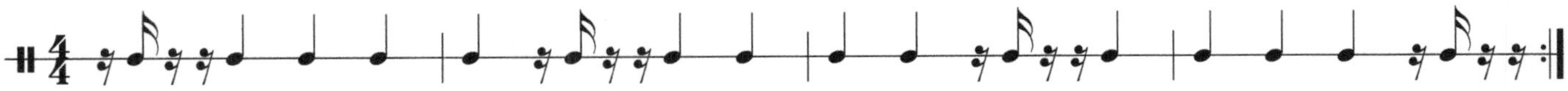

13. 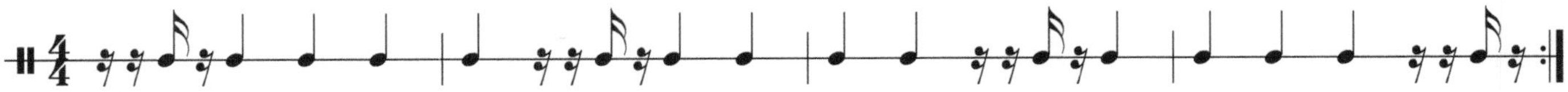

14. 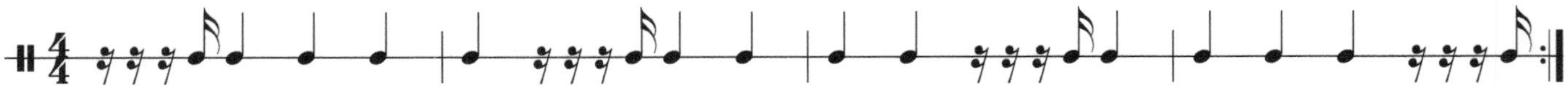

15. 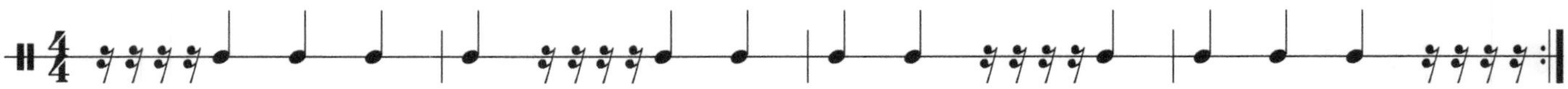

Long and Short Notes

Below are a series of two-measure exercises. Each measure (on each line) sounds almost the same, with the exception that one rhythm contains notes of shorter duration (i.e., measure 1 and measure 2 of each line). For the purpose of this exercise, play the reference measure first, followed by exercise 1, followed by the reference measure, then exercise 2, etc. The purpose of the reference measure/line is to simply serve as a starting point for the exercises you'll be playing. Some of the reference measures/lines may contain elements of the rhythms that follow, and others will not as they simply function as a starting point. These reference measures/lines will help you look ahead when moving from one part of the page to the next. Pay careful attention to the correct release of the notes on the first measure of each line.

Tied Notes

Tied notes can be defined in a variety of ways. Basically, a tied note is one that is tied to another (one that immediately follows the note that is tied). It lengthens a note by the use of a curved line. Below are some examples of how ties are used and the rhythms they represent. Sometimes ties are written to make certain passages easier to read and perform.

Triplet Exercises in 4/4

In the following exercises, the triplet is played in groups of one, two, three and four, all with and without rests.
Repeat each measure as many times as you'd like. You can also go back and forth from the first measure of each
exercise to any other measure within that exercise.

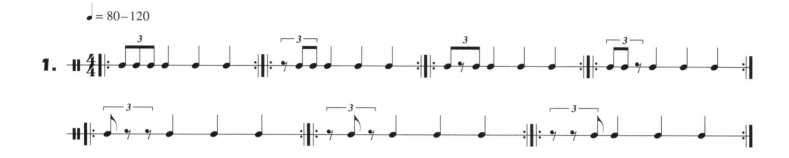

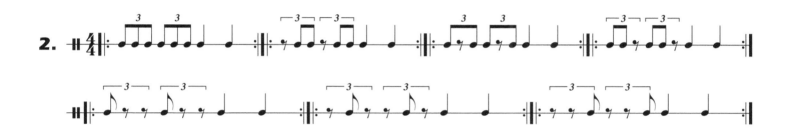

Combining Triplets with Rests (Groups of Two)

Here comes the fun! Now that you've gotten the triplet "feel" under your belt, let's try it again in groups of two. Try using your breath during the rests in order to help you feel the pulse of the triplet figure. You can also set your metronome to a triplet subdivision setting. Play the reference line between each exercise.

1. **2.**

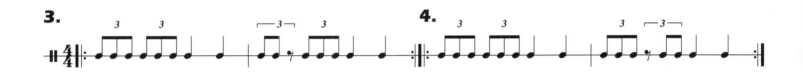

3. **4.**

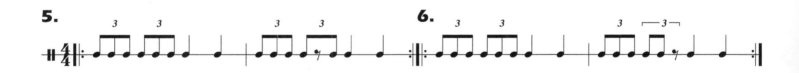

5. **6.**

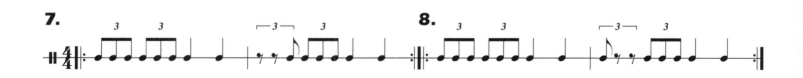

7. **8.**

9. **10.**

11.

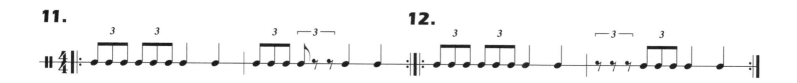

12.

13.

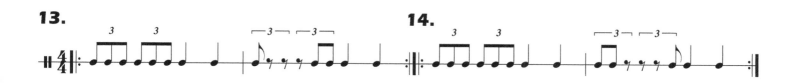

14.

15.

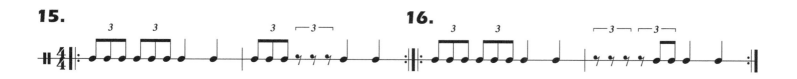

16.

17.

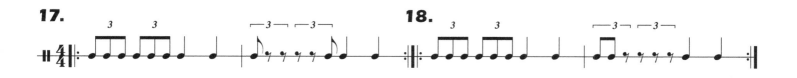

18.

19.

20.

21.

The Quarter-Note Triplet

Below are exercises to help assist you in learning the quarter-note triplet. These exercises contain the eighth-note triplet subdivision. Before playing through the entire page, practice exercise 1 until you're comfortable with the rhythm.

Now, go back and play it again. This time, however, play the triplets as tied figures (see exercise 2). If you'd like, add a slight accent to every tied note in order to emphasize the quarter-note triplet.

By playing exercise 2, you are also playing the same rhythm as exercise 3.

3.

You are now ready to play exercises 1, 2 and 3. This time, however, you will play them back to back (see exercise 4).

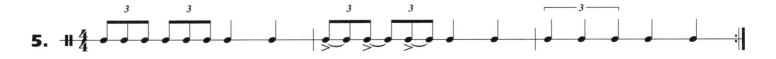

In exercise 4, the quarter-note triplet occurs on beats 3 and 4. In exercise 5, the quarter-note triplet occurs on beats 1 and 2. Remember, the quarter-note triplets occur in the span of two quarter-note beats. As before, play each measure separately, then one after the other.

Exercise 6 contains a quarter-note triplet that falls in the middle of the measure (beats 2 and 3). This rhythm might feel weird at first, but it is played just like the previous quarter-note triplets except that it falls on two different beats.

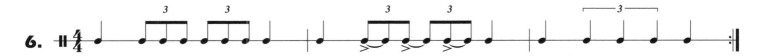

Always remember that rhythms are patterns. The key to better rhythm reading is to practice rhythm exercises the same as you would scale patterns.

Understanding Quarter-Note Triplets

A quarter-note triplet occurs within the space of two quarter-note beats. In the following exercises, we are going to perform quarter-note triplets with the addition of eighth notes as part of the quarter-note triplet figure. I have included the use of the eighth-note triplet subdivision (with ties) to assist in the execution of the quarter-note triplet.

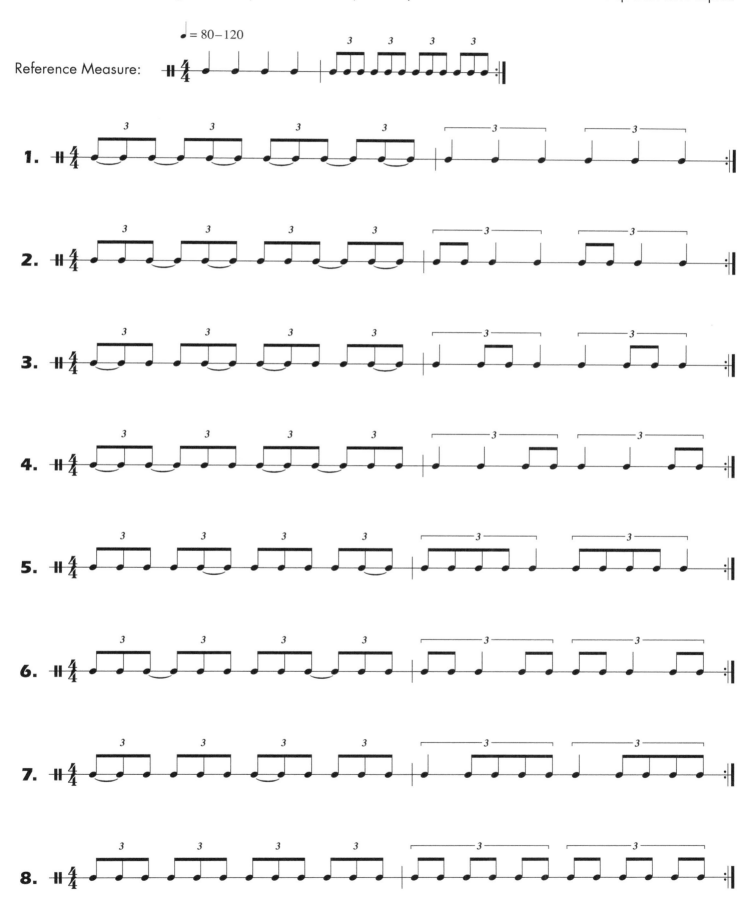

Quarter-Note Triplets with Rests

Beats 1 and 2

Here, the quarter-note triplets and rests occur on beats 1 and 2. Even though exercise 7 starts with the quarter-note triplet as a rest, it is important that you "feel" the triplet during the silence. This process will come in handy when applying eighth notes as part of the triplet rhythm. Play the reference measure first, followed by exercise 1, and so on.

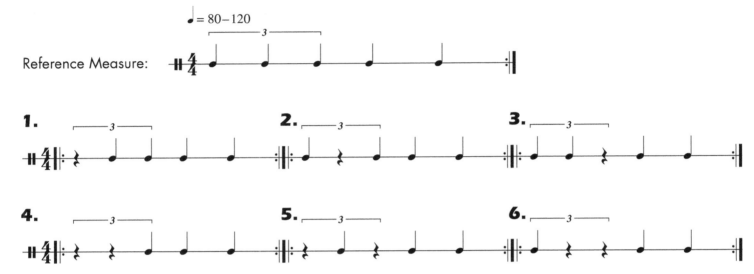

Beats 2 and 3

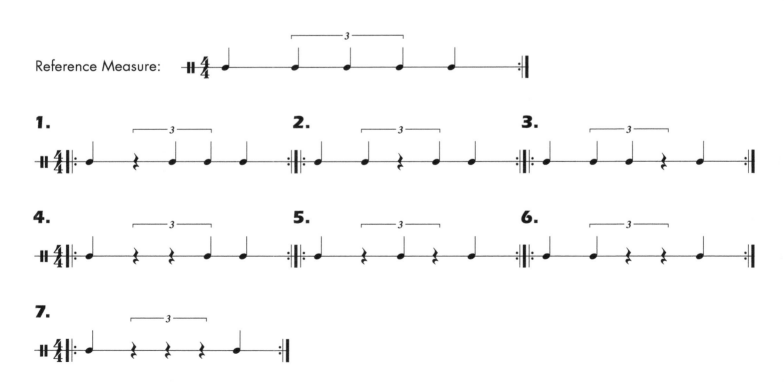

Quarter-Note Triplets with Eighth-Note Patterns

Beats 2 and 3

Beats 3 and 4

Quarter-Note Triplets with Eighth-Note Patterns

Beats 1 and 2

The rhythms on this page are not as common as those found on the previous pages. Sometimes performers will have to stop and examine the rhythm before playing it. Practicing these exercises on a daily basis will help you avoid hesitation when encountering the following rhythms. Practice these and all exercises at various tempos, but start slowly at first to ensure accurate rhythmic execution.

For the purpose of these exercises, the quarter-note triplet figure (with eighth notes) occurs on beats 1 and 2. I have used tied notes to help you visualize the exact placement of the eighth notes. If you'd like, you can place a slight accent on the tied notes to help you "feel" the triplet rhythm. Play the reference measure first, followed by exercise 1, and so on.

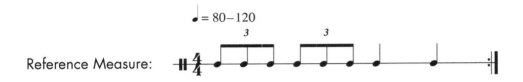

Reference Measure:

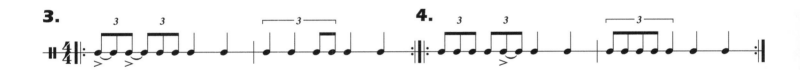

Quarter-Note Triplets with Rests

Beats 3 and 4

Now that you're comfortable with quarter-note triplets, let's add some rests to the quarter-note triplet figure. Remember, now that we are applying silence (rests) as part of the rhythm, it's important to "feel" the subdivision. Make sure to release the sound exactly where the rest occurs.

Quarter-Note Triplets with Half Notes and Rests

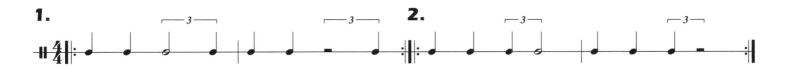

Quarter-Note Triplets with Eighth-Note Patterns

Beats 1–2 and 3–4

Now that you've practiced placing a quarter-note triplet (two-beat triplet) within various parts of the measure, we will now practice the equivalent of two quarter-note triplets within an entire measure of $\frac{4}{4}$. It's important to note that the quarter-note triplet can also occur within odd meters. Remember, it's just a pattern. Recognize it and play it!

16th-Note Triplets

The 16th-note triplet falls in the span of an eighth note. A set of 16th-note triplets has been placed on each eighth-note subdivision of the measure. Repeat each line as many times as you wish. For timing purposes, we will begin with quarter notes (in the reference line), then eighths, followed by 16th-note triplets. When you're ready, play just the second measures of each exercise straight down. You can also jump from the second measure of the first exercise, to the second measure of the fifth exercise, to the second measure of the seventh exercise, and so on.

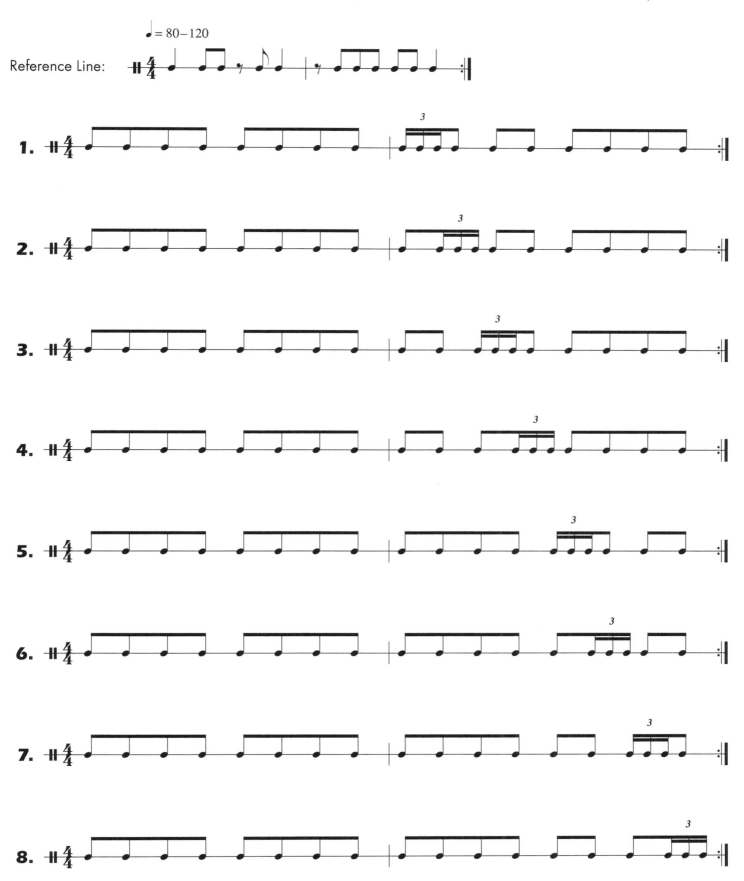

Sextuplet Exercises

A sextuplet can be defined as two 16th-note triplets performed back-to-back (two consecutive eighth notes). The exercises on this page consist of a sextuplet performed both on and off each beat of a measure. For timing purposes, each exercise will begin with a reference line. To help you keep steady time, set your metronome to an eighth-note subdivision. When you're ready, play just the second measures of each exercise straight down. You can also start on the second measure of exercise seven and play the second measure of each exercise straight up, or just jump from the second measure of one exercise to another.

Two-Beat Sextuplet Exercises

We are now going to do a series of two sextuplets within a measure. These can also be performed both on and off the beat. For timing purposes, each line will begin with two measures of groove, followed by a measure of eighth notes, followed by the measure with the set of two sextuplets. To keep from rushing or dragging, set your metronome to an eighth-note subdivision. When you're ready, play just the fourth measure of each exercise straight down. You can also start on the fourth measure of exercise five, and play the fourth measure of each line straight up.

Figure 1:

As before, play the fourth measure of each exercise straight down and in various other combinations. Also, place an eighth-note rest before and after each combination of sextuplets (see figure 1). You can also try resting through the entire fourth measure of each exercise, except where a pair of sextuplets occurs.

Three-Beat Sextuplet Exercises

For the exercises below, we are going to apply the use of three sextuplet figures that occur both on and off the beat. For timing purposes, each line will begin with two measures of groove, followed by a measure of eighth notes, followed by the measure with the set of three sextuplets. To keep from rushing or dragging, set your metronome to an eighth-note subdivision. When you're ready, play just the fourth measure of each exercise straight down. You can also start on the fourth measure of exercise three, and play the fourth measure of each exercise straight up.

The following exercise contains four consecutive sextuplets in the fourth measure.

It's important to note that although there are many exercises that include the sextuplet figure, there are just as many that include sextuplets with rests.

The more you practice sextuplets, the easier it will be to play them when they contain rests.

Beat Cells

On the following pages, you will find a series of "beat cells." A beat cell is basically one beat's worth of a particular rhythm placed in a circle, hence the name cell. The goal is to be able to read at least "one beat ahead." The arrows found in each exercise are used to provide possible variations when performing these exercises.

Here is how the beat-cell exercises work.

- Play the beat cells along with a metronome or to one of the tracks on the enclosed CD.

- Set your metronome to a tempo slow enough for you to be able to play one beat cell while looking at another.

- Play each beat cell four times before moving on to the next one.

- Play each beat cell three times before moving on to the next one.

- Play each beat cell two times before moving on to the next one.

- Play each beat cell only once and jump to another one.

- Do not stop—**even if you play a wrong rhythm.**

- Follow all possible variations provided by the arrows.

- Try jumping from one page to the next.

- Train your eyes to take a picture of the beat cell (rhythm), and memorize it!

Once you've completed this section of the book, you will notice a drastic improvement in your sight-reading ability. **Have fun.**

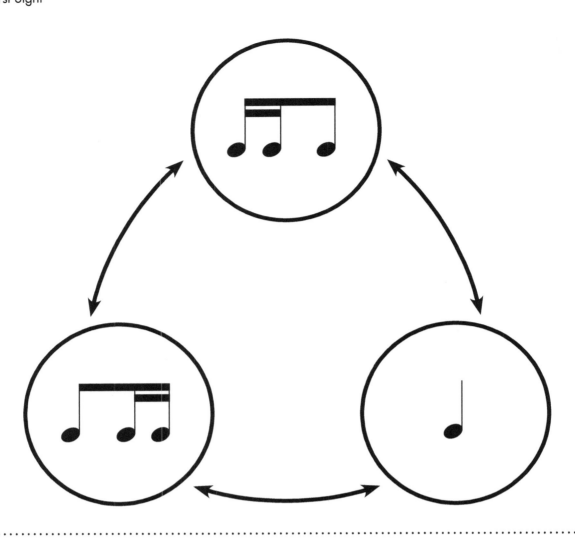

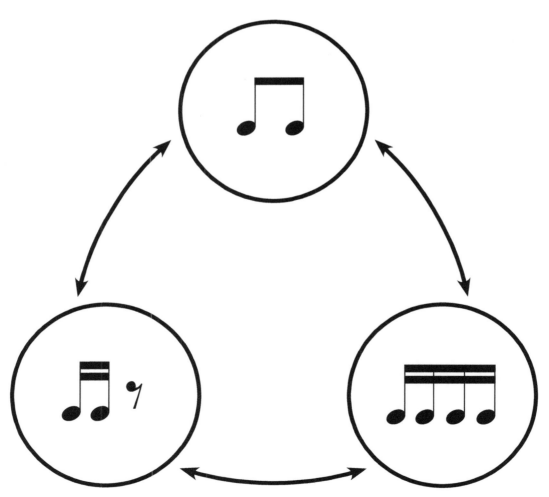

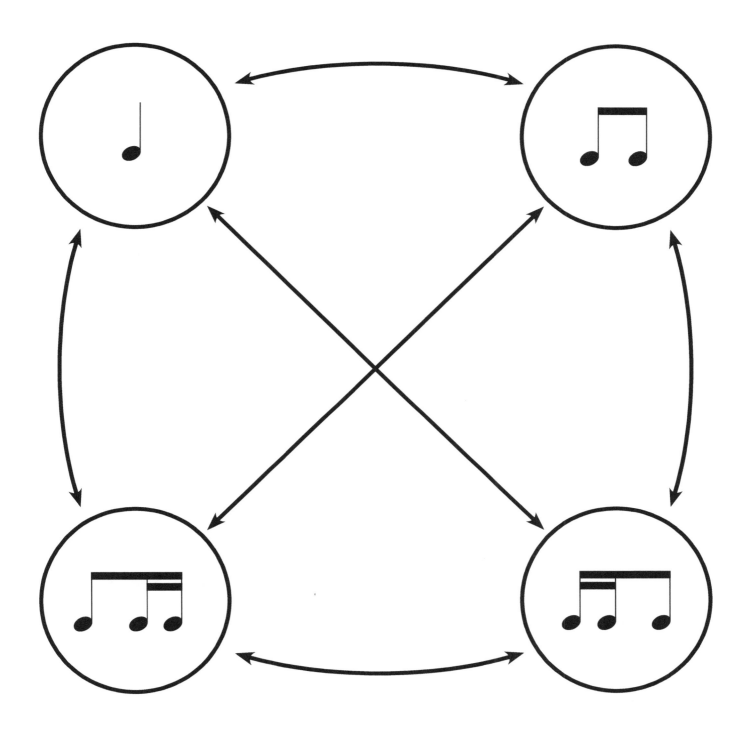

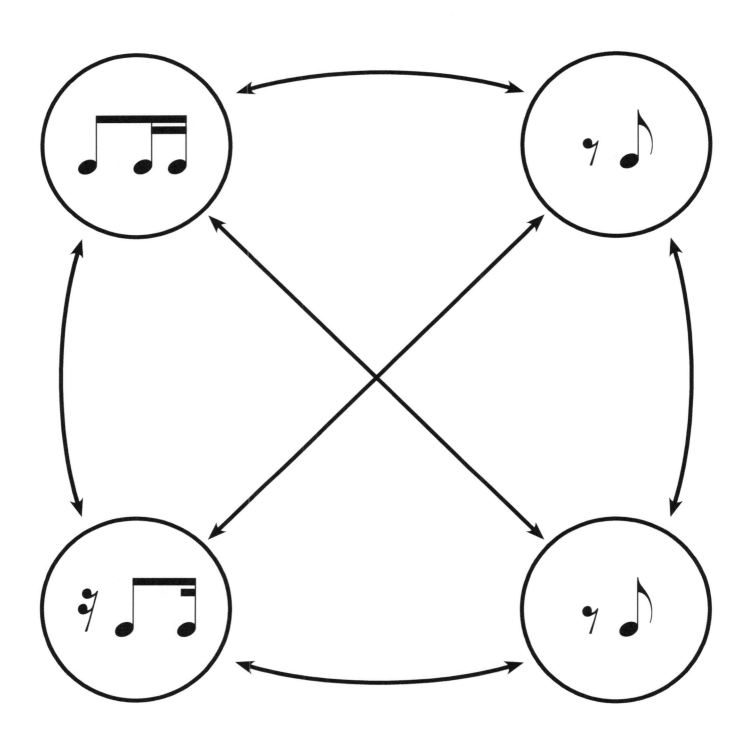

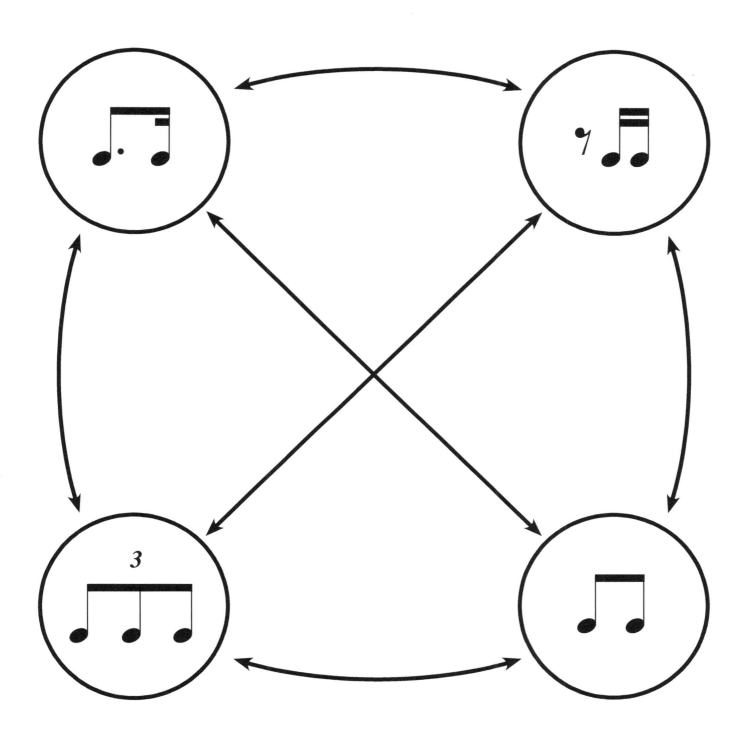

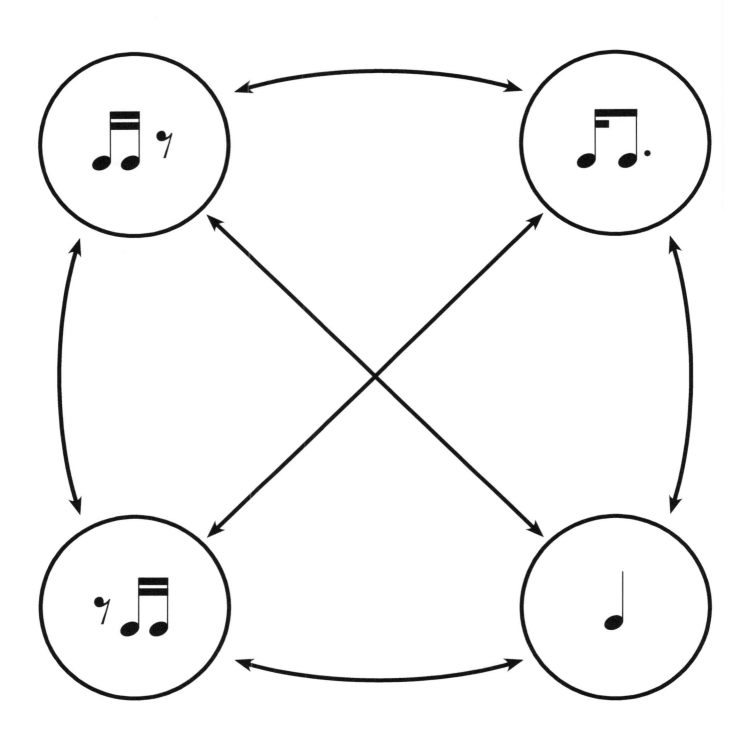

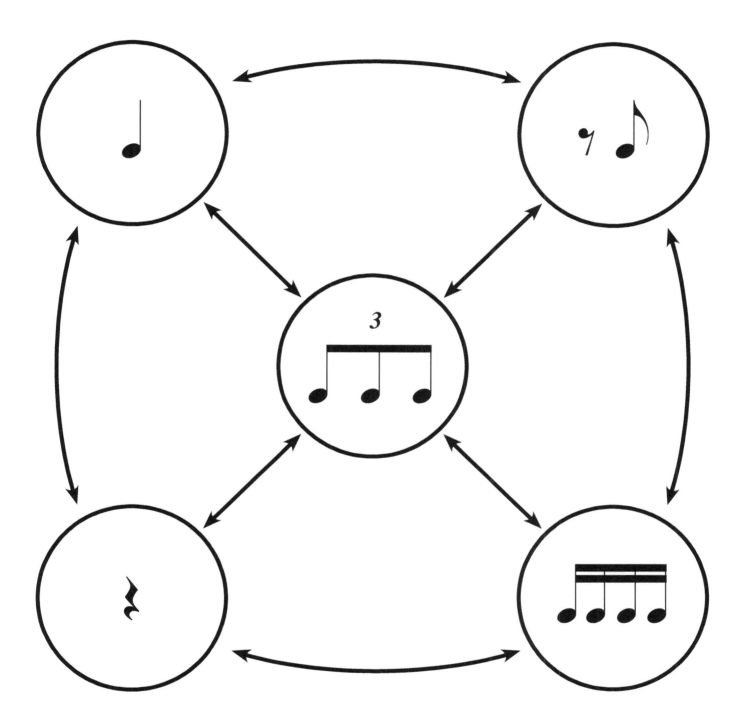

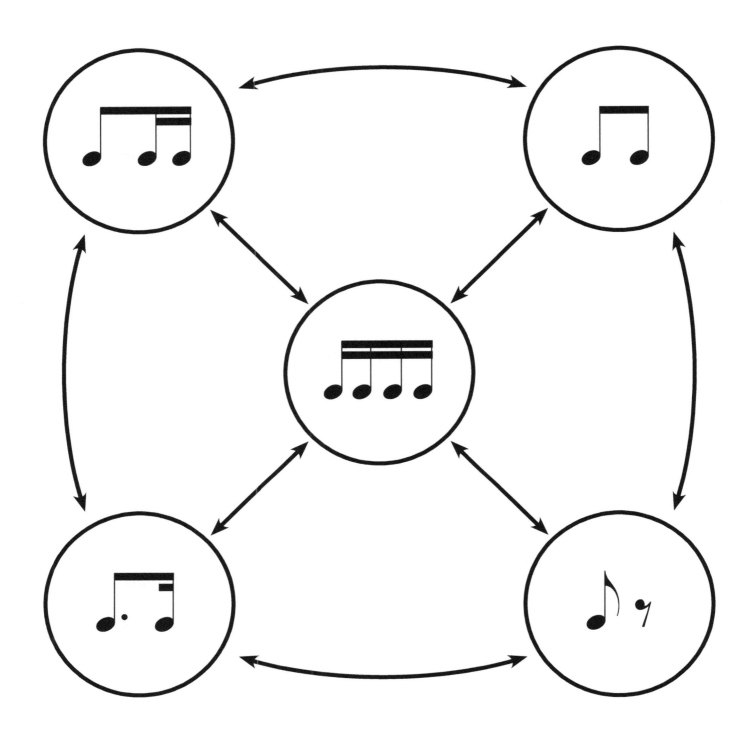

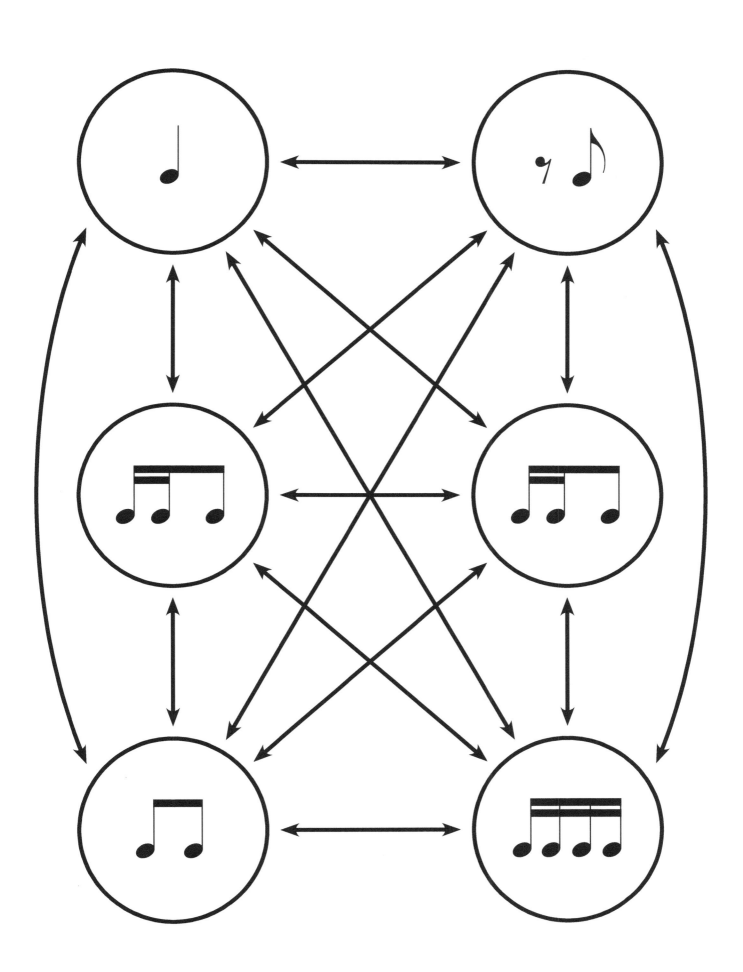

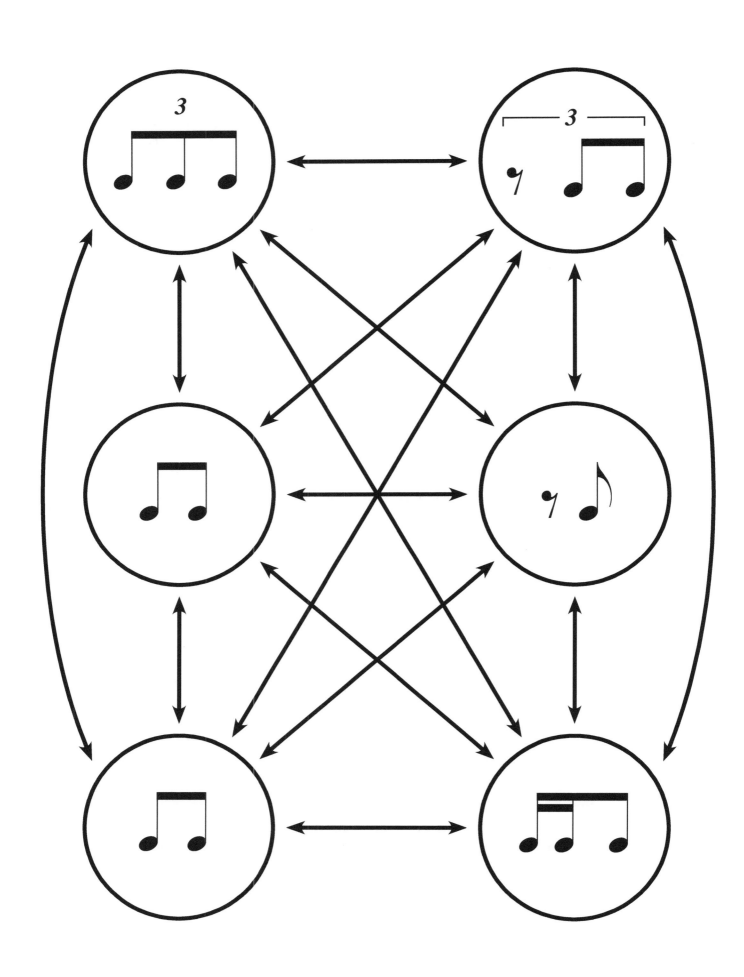

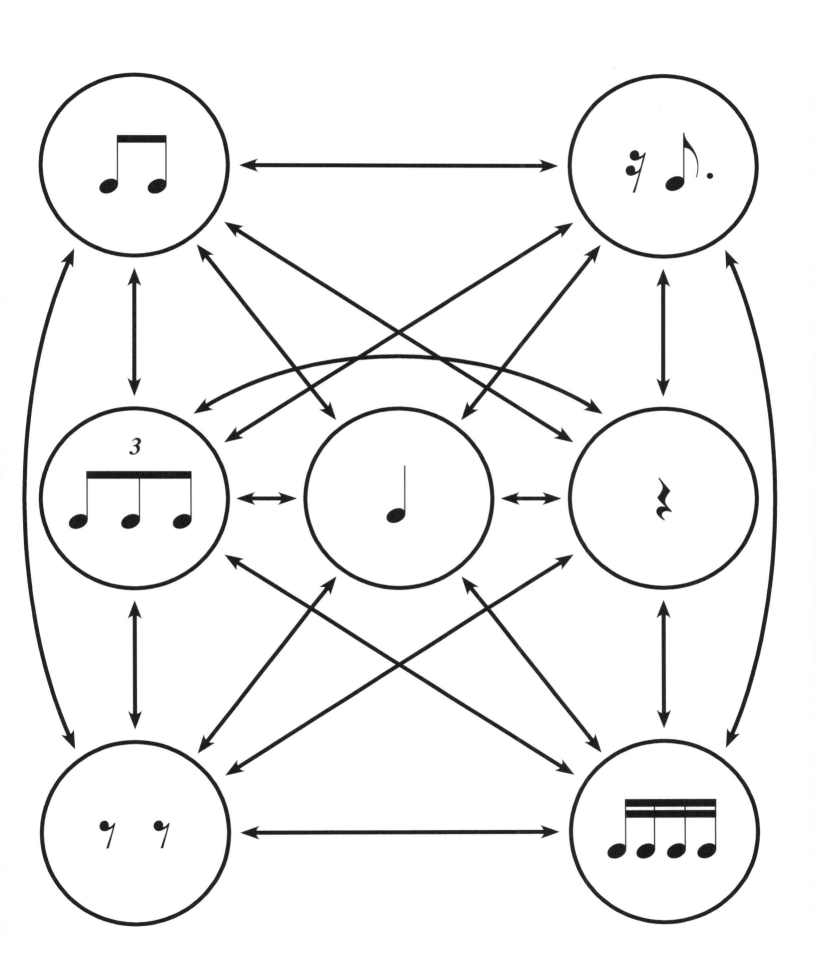

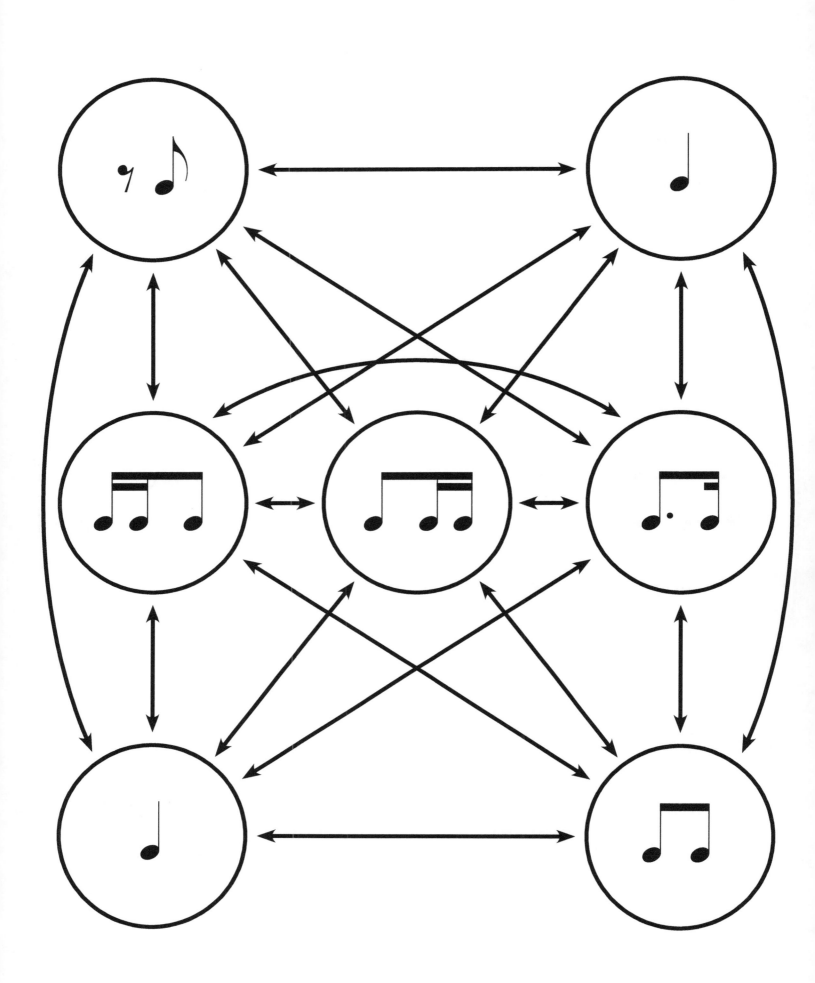

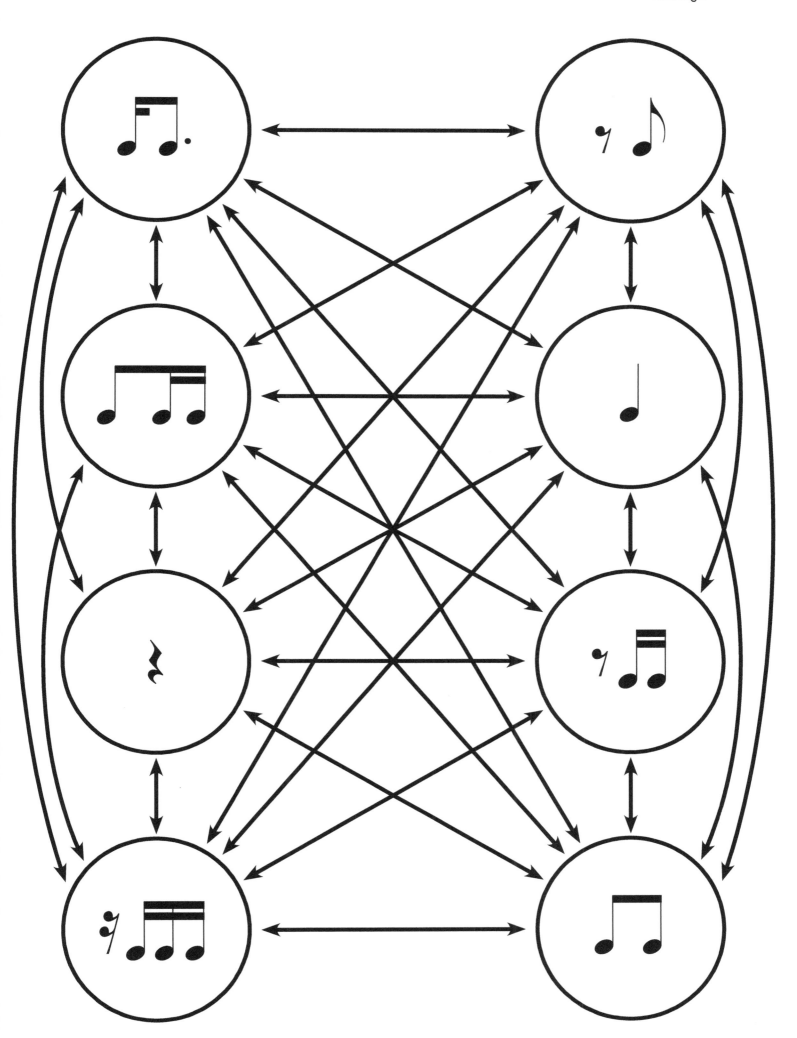

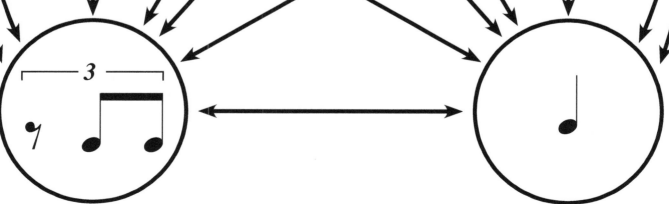

Jump-Around Measure Exercises

In the next few pages, you will find a series of two- , three- , four- , five- , six- , seven- , and eight-measure exercises. These exercises are probably unlike any you've ever done before. I've purposely separated the measures in an effort to force you to literally **"look ahead."**

By the time you've reached this page, you should have played through all the previous exercises. If not, I highly recommend you go back and play through all the exercises prior to this section – particularly those that contain "reference measures." If you recall, you were asked to memorize the reference measures first, then perform them between each exercise without having to go back and look at them each time. Again, the goal is to **"look ahead."** Looking ahead is exactly what I want you to do in the following exercises. This section functions the same as the "beat-cell" section, except we are now working with full measures instead of just beats. We will start with two-measure exercises.

Here is what you do.

- Set the metronome to a tempo you feel comfortable working with.

- Use four counts up front to get started (memorize the first measure during those four counts).

- If you need to go back and work on the "beat-cell" section, go ahead.

- Go back and forth from one measure to another. While playing one measure, your eyes should be looking ahead to another measure (great for learning to read ahead).

- Before moving on, stay on a page until you feel you've mastered it.

Since we are only working with two measures in the first part of this section, there aren't as many variations that can be applied. As the number of measures increase, so will the number of possible variations. For an additional challenge in the two measure jump-around portion of this book, try playing beats 1 and 3, and then beats 2 and 4 of each measure. Again, the purpose is to "look ahead."

Two Measure Jump-Around Exercises

Here, you will do exactly what the title suggests, and jump around from one measure to another. Below you will find four, two measure jump-around exercises. Again, the measures have been purposely separated in order to force you to practice memorizing the measures while looking ahead. Remember, while performing one measure, your eyes should be looking ahead to the measure about to be performed. With this set of exercises, you're limited to only playing two measures. As the number of measures increase, so will the number of variations and the challenge of jumping from measure to measure.

♩ = 80–120

No. 1

No. 2

No. 3

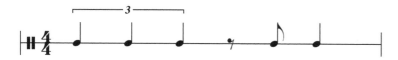

No. 4

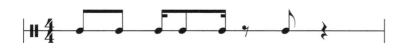

Three Measure Jump-Around Exercises

Below are four, three measure jump-around exercises. Here, the same concept as with the two measure jump-around exercises is applied. The addition of one measure to these exercises increases the variation possibilities. So, while playing measure 1, your eyes should be looking ahead to measure 2. While playing measure 2, your eyes should be looking ahead to measure 3. Finally, while playing measure 3, your eyes should be looking ahead to measure 1. You can also start this exercise by playing measure 2 first, followed by measure 3, etc., or you can choose to perform them in any order you like.

♩ = 80–120

No. 1

No. 2

No. 3

No. 4

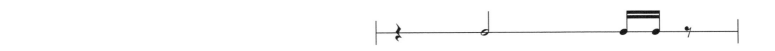

Four Measure Jump-Around Exercises

Below are four, four measure jump-around exercises. Here, the same concept as with the three measure jump-around exercises is applied. The addition of one measure to each exercise increases the variation possibilities. So, while playing measure 1, your eyes should be looking ahead to measure 2. While playing measure 2, your eyes should be looking ahead to measure 3, and so on. Finally, while playing measure 4, your eyes should be looking ahead to measure 1, and so on. You can also start this exercise by playing measure 2 first, followed by measure 3, etc., or you can choose to perform them in any order you like.

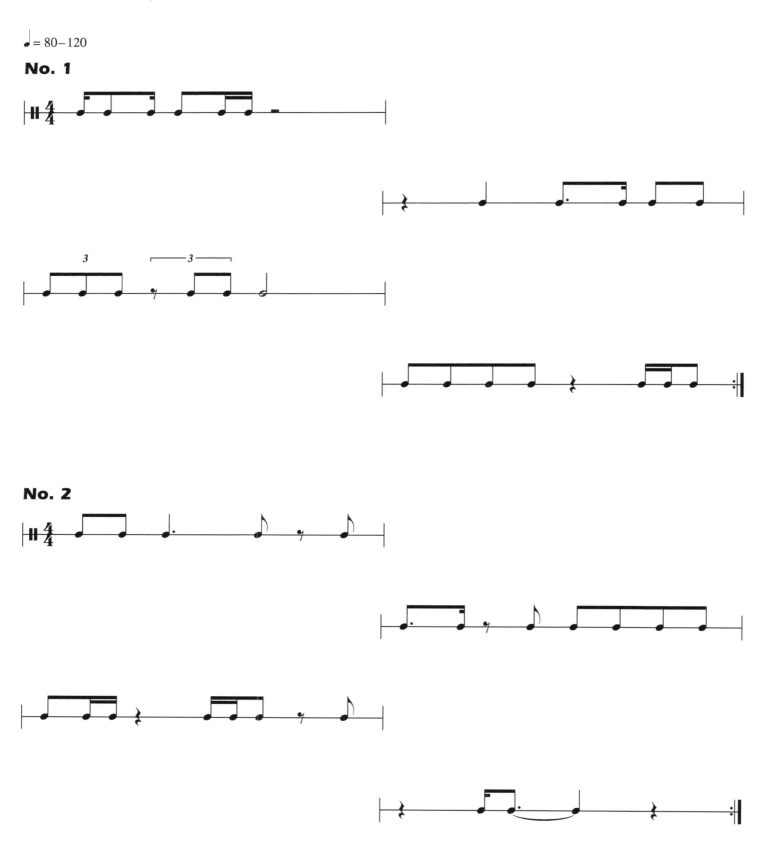

No. 3

No. 4

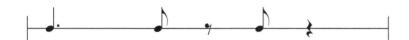

Five Measure Jump-Around Exercises

Below are four, five measure jump-around exercises. Here, the same concept is applied as with the four measure jump-around exercises. The addition of one measure to each exercise increases the variation possibilities. So, while playing measure 1, your eyes should be looking ahead to measure 2. While playing measure 2, your eyes should be looking ahead to measure 3, and so on. Finally, while playing measure 5, your eyes should be looking ahead to measure 1, and so on. You can also start this exercise by playing measure 2 first, followed by measure 3, etc., or you can choose to perform them in any order you like.

♩ = 80–120

No. 1

No. 2

No. 3

No. 4

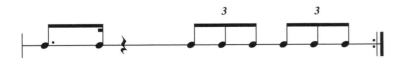

Six Measure Jump-Around Exercises

Below are four, six measure jump-around exercises. Here, the same concept is applied as with the five measure jump-around exercises. The addition of one measure to that exercise increases the variation possibilities. So, while playing measure 1, your eyes should be looking ahead to measure 2. While playing measure 2, your eyes should be looking ahead to measure 3, and so on. Finally, while playing measure 6, your eyes should be looking ahead to measure 1 and so on. You can also start this exercise by playing measure 2 first, followed by measure 3, etc., or you can choose to perform them in any order you like.

♩ = 80–120

No. 1

No. 2

No. 3

No. 4

Seven Measure Jump-Around Exercises

Below are four, seven measure jump-around exercises. Here, the same concept is applied as with the six measure jump-around exercises. The addition of one measure to each exercise increases the variation possibilities. So, while playing measure 1, your eyes should be looking ahead to measure 2. While playing measure 2, your eyes should be looking ahead to measure 3, and so on. Finally, while playing measure 7, your eyes should be looking ahead to measure 1, and so on. You can also start this exercise by playing measure 2 first, followed by measure 3, etc., or you can choose to perform them in any order you like.

♩ = 80–120

No. 1

No. 2

No. 3

No. 4

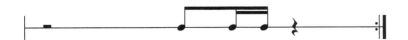

Eight Measure Jump-Around Exercises

Below are four, eight measure jump-around exercises. Here, the same concept is applied as with the seven measure jump-around exercises. The addition of one measure to each exercise increases the variation possibilities. So, while playing measure 1, your eyes should be looking ahead to measure 2. While playing measure 2, your eyes should be looking ahead to measure 3, and so on. Finally, while playing measure 8, your eyes should be looking ahead to measure 1, and so on. You can also start this exercise by playing measure 2 first, followed by measure 3, etc., or you can choose to perform them in any order you like.

♩ = 80–120

No. 1

No. 2

No. 3

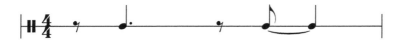
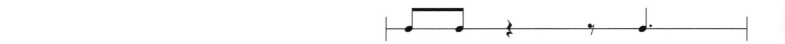

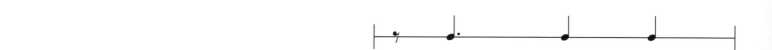
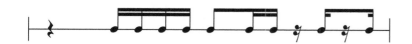

No. 4

Bar None

Now that you've completed the section on "beat cells" and jump-around exercises, I want you to try and perform the following exercises. Notice that the bar lines have been omitted in this section of the book, hence the title "Bar None." The exercises are actually 40-bars long, with a total of 80 bars if each line is repeated (in $\frac{4}{4}$ time). You can play these exercises along with either a metronome (start slowly) or with any of the CD tracks in $\frac{4}{4}$ time. Hopefully you won't find these exercises difficult to perform as you've already spent a lot of time practicing your beat-cell exercises.

Each of the bar-none exercises consist of a single-line staff. When applying notes to the exercises, the rhythm below the line should be played using the tonic/root of the chord in the key of the CD track. For the rhythms above the line, play the dominant/fifth of the chord.

I recommend playing the following exercises as such.

- Play with a metronome set to a slow tempo.

- Repeat each line as many times as you wish.

- When you feel like you're ready, pick a track from the enclosed CD and play the exercises along with that track.

- If you play to a track, you must use the repeats.

- Once you've completed a "bar-none" exercise, it's time to start jumping around from line-to-line within an exercise.

- Be patient! This study will definitely pay off.

Bar None 1

Bar None 2

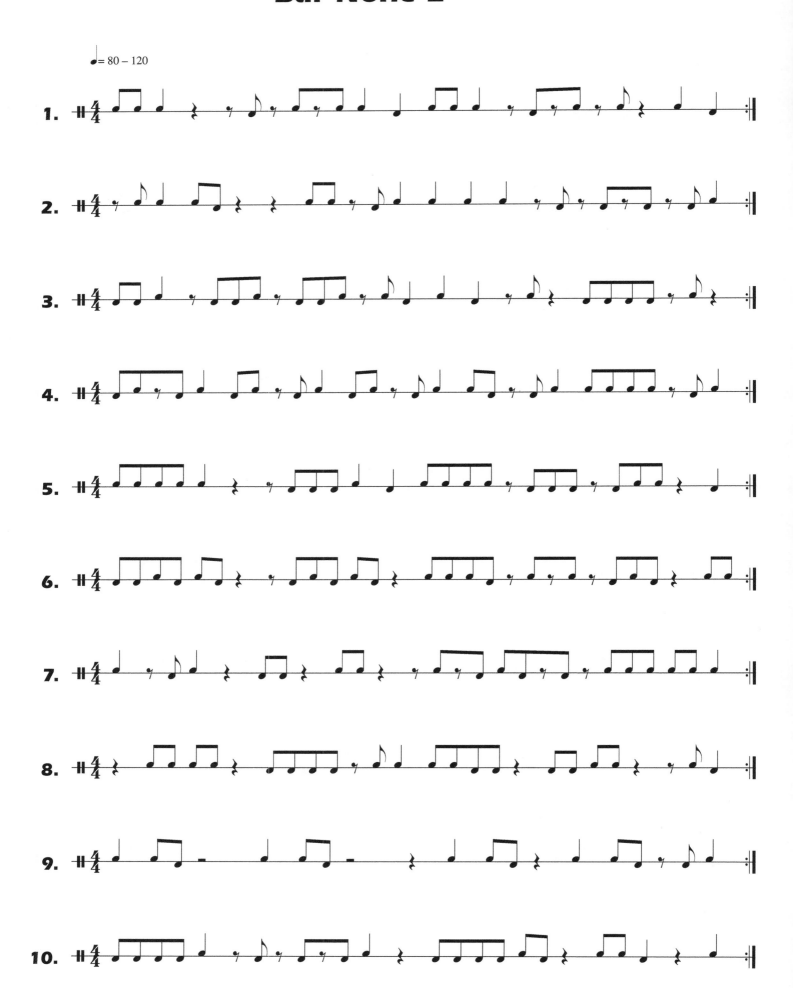

Bar None 3

Bar None 4

♩ = 80 – 120

Bar None 5

Congratulations

You are now ready to perform the "study" section of this book. Please refer to the variation page, located in the Appendix, when working on the 42 studies. The tracks on the enclosed CD are to be used with these studies. You may use the tracks to work on other sections of the book as well. The music on the CD consists of various musical styles. Though no special articulations have been included in these 42 studies, I highly encourage you to experiment with numerous articulations common to their instrument/voice. As for dynamics, those too have been left out. As you get comfortable with each study, feel free to add dynamics to any section of the music.

Have fun!

When you're done with the entire book, turn the book upside down and start over. ☺

The Process for Performing the 42 Studies

All of the studies can be performed with any of the tracks on the enclosed CD. The following exercises/studies will work with any track, except for those written in an odd-time meter. Those exercises will have their own tracks. Each exercise is 80 measures long. The tracks on the CD are also 80 measures long, with a release on the downbeat. Each track will begin with a two-measure introduction.

Here are some ways in which to perform/read the following exercises/studies.

- First, read the page straight down (with repeats). Play each exercise along with a track on the enclosed CD.

- Next, read the page straight down again, only this time with no repeats per exercise. When you're finished playing exercise 10, jump back to exercise one and play it down again.

- Now, on that same page, read (with repeats) all the odd numbers first (i.e. 1, 3, 5, 7, 9), then read the even numbers (2, 4, 6, 8, 10).

- Now, play all the odd numbers with no repeats, followed by all the even numbers with no repeats, followed by odd and even again, so the exercise equals 80 measures.

Study 1

Study 2

Study 3

Study 4

Study 5

Study 6

Study 7

Study 8

Study 9

Study 10

Study 11

Study 12

♩= 80 – 120

Study 13

♩ = 80 – 120

Study 14

Study 15

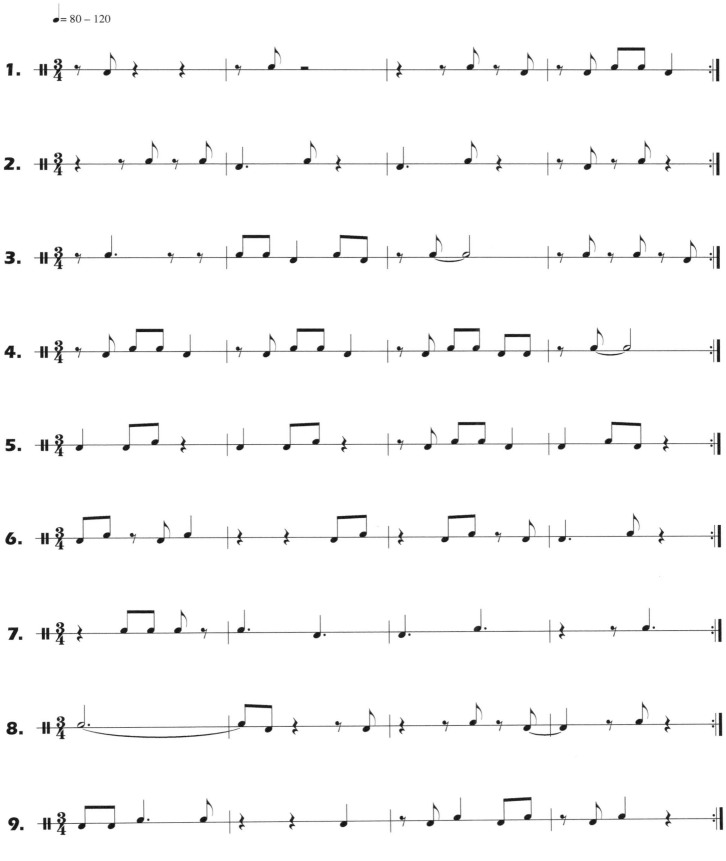

Study 16

♩ = 80 – 120

Study 17

♩ = 80 – 120

Study 18

Study 21

Study 22

Study 23

Study 24

Study 25

Study 26

Study 27

Study 28

Study 29

Study 30

Study 31

Study 32

Study 33

Study 34

♩ = 80 – 120

Study 35

Study 36

Study 37

Study 38

Study 39

Study 40

Study 41

Study 42

Closing Remarks

I believe by using this book as part of your daily practice routine, your confidence in sight-reading rhythms will improve tremendously. Just remember to "always look ahead." Once you feel like you can perform the entire book utilizing the fifth and root of each track, feel free to try jumping around the root, third, and fifth. Once you're comfortable with that, try incorporating the entire scale of each track. Basically, the sky is the limit. The whole point is to read rhythms and "have fun." It is my hope that this book will help everyone become better sight-readers and, therefore, better musicians.

Appendix

Variations on Performing the 42 Studies

A. Straight down with repeats.

B. Straight down with no repeats, but played twice.

C. All even numbers with repeats – all odd numbers with repeats.

D. All even numbers with no repeats (played twice), followed by all odd numbers with no repeats (played twice).

E. Start with exercise 10, followed by exercises 9, 8, 7, 6, 5, 4, 3, 2 and 1 with repeats.

F. Exercises 10, 9, 8, 7, 6, 5, 4, 3, 2 and 1 with no repeats, but played twice.

G. All even numbers, with repeats played twice.

H. All odd numbers, with repeats played twice.

I. Exercises 10, 8, 6, 4 and 2 played with repeats – then exercises 9, 7, 5, 3 and 1 played with repeats.

J. Exercises 10, 8, 6, 4, 2, 9, 7, 5, 3 and 1 played with repeats.

K. Exercises 10, 8, 6, 4, 2, 9, 7, 5, 3 and 1 played twice, without repeats.

L. Play the first measure of each exercise (1–10), then jump up to the second measure of exercise one and play all the second measures straight down. Go up to the third measure of the first exercise and play all the third measures straight down. Go up to the fourth measure of the first exercise and play all the fourth measures straight down. Go back to the first measure of exercise one and repeat the process. This should equal 80 bars.

M. Beginning with line one, play all the first measures of each exercise (1–10). When you play the first measure of exercise 10, move to the second measure of exercise 10 and play all the second measures going up (i.e., 10, 9, 8, 7, 6, 5, 4, 3, 2 and 1). When you play the second measure of exercise one, play the third measure of the same exercise and then play all the third measures straight down (i.e., 1, 2, 3, 4, 5, 6, 7, 8, 9, and 10). When you get to the third measure of line 10, play the fourth measure of the same line and then play all the fourth measures straight up to exercise 1. When you play the fourth measure of line 1, go back and repeat the entire process. This should equal 80 bars.

N. Play all the first measures of each exercise starting with exercise 1. After playing the first measure of exercise 10, jump up to line one and play the third measure of exercise 1 and all the third measures of each exercise straight down. After you play the third measure of exercise 10, jump up and play the second measure of exercise 1 and all the second measures of each exercise straight down. When you play the second measure of exercise 10, go up to line one and play the fourth measure of exercise 1 and all the fourth measures of each exercise straight down. When you play the fourth measure of exercise 10, go back to line one and repeat the process.

O. Same process as letter N, except start on measure 2 of exercise 1, then measure 4, then measure 1, and then measure 3. Come up with your own variations of letter N.

P. Same process as letters N & O, except start on exercise 10 instead of line one.

Q. Now to get your eyes to look ahead even further, try the following: Play the first measure of exercise 1, followed by the third measure, followed by the second measure, followed by the fourth, then repeat exercise 1. Do this with each exercise.

R. Same as letter Q, except in this exercise order: 1, 3, 5, 7, 9, 2, 4, 6, 8 and 10, with and without repeats. Remember, when you play an exercise without the written repeats, you must play it twice for it to equal 80 measures.

S. Same as letters Q & R, except start on measure 2, then measure 4, then measure 1, followed by measure 3. Come up with your own combinations.

T. Play measure 1 of exercise 1, followed by measure 4, followed by measure 2, followed by measure 3. Do this for each exercise, both with and without repeats.

U. Here is a hard one for you. Start on exercise 1 and play measures 1–4. When you get to measure 4 of exercise 1, jump to the fourth measure of exercise 2 and play measures 4–1 of exercise 2. When you get to the first measure of exercise 2, jump to the first measure of exercise 3 and play measures 1–4, etc. Do this until you've completed the entire page, both with and without repeats.

V. Same as letter U, except start on exercise 10.

W. Try exercise 1, then exercise 10; exercise 2, then exercise 9; exercise 3, then exercise 8; exercise 4, then exercise 7; exercise 5, followed by exercise 6. Do this both with and without repeats. Remember to "look ahead."

X. Start with exercise 1, but play the measures in this order: 4, 3, 2, and 1. Do the same for each of the other exercises, both with and without repeats.

Y. Here is another good idea. Play measure 1 of exercise 1, but do not play measure 2 (make measure 2 a full measure of rest). Play measure 3, but do not play measure 4 (make measure 4 a full measure of rest). Doing it this way will give you four beats of rest to prepare for the next rhythm. Apply the same idea for each of the other exercises, both with and without repeats.

Z. The same as letter Y, except do not play measure 1 (make measure 1 a full measure of rest). Play measure 2, but do not play measure 3 (make measure 3 a full measure of rest). Apply the same idea for each exercise, with and without repeats. Jump from line-to-line and come up with your own variations.

As you can see, I have come up with at least 26 variations for each exercise. There are endless possibilities. Remember, take a mental picture of the rhythm you're playing and, while you are playing that rhythm, your eyes should be looking at least one measure ahead to prepare for the next rhythm.

The best way to feel more comfortable and confident with your rhythm-reading skills is to practice the exercises in this book on a regular basis. Make rhythm practicing part of your daily-practice routine. A good 5 to 15 minutes per practice session will drastically improve your sight-reading abilities. Obviously, the more time you spend sight-reading, the better and more proficient you will become.

How to Apply the 42 Studies
to Each Instrument

➤ Wind Players

- Use articulations from the articulation section of this book.

- Play all of the rhythms on one pitch first.

- For rhythms below the line, play the root of the chord.

- For rhythms above the line, play the fifth of the chord.

- Come up with your own application of dynamics.

➤ Pianists

- Play the rhythms below the line with your left hand using the root of the key.

- Play the rhythms above the line with your right hand using the fifth of the key.

- Groove with the left hand, and play the rhythms with the right hand.

- Groove with the right hand, and play the rhythms with the left hand.

- Groove for a measure, play the rhythms in the next measure, and so on.

- Groove with the tracks while singing the rhythms.

- Play and sing the rhythms at the same time.

➤ Bass Guitar

- Play the notes below the line using the root of the chord.

- Play the notes above the line using the fifth of the chord.

- Groove for a measure, play the rhythms in the next measure, and so on.

- Groove with the tracks while singing the rhythms.

- Play and sing the rhythms at the same time.

➤ String Players

- Same as the bass guitar.

➤ Drumset

- Play the downbeats with the right hand on the hi-hat. The left hand plays the notes above the line on the snare drum and below the line on the bass drum. Where fast rhythms occur below the line, you can use a double bass-drum pedal or play the rhythms between the snare drum and bass drum.

- Same as above, except in reverse order.

- Where long notes occur, combine (hit at the same time) a cymbal with either a snare- or bass-drum note.

- Groove for a measure, play the rhythms in the next measure, and so on.

- Try playing along with the grooves of each track while playing the written figures.

Percussionists can also benefit from using this book in the following manner:

➤ Congas

- Play the rhythms above the line using the high drum, and the rhythms below the line using the low drum.
- Play the rhythms above the line using the low drum, and the rhythms below the line using the high drum.
- Use a mounted cowbell (with foot pedal) to play the downbeats, while playing the figures on the congas.
- Groove for a measure, play the rhythms in the next measure, and so on.
- Play rolls for long notes.
- Groove with the tracks while singing the rhythms.

➤ Timbales or Bongos

- Follow the same formula as with the congas.

➤ Timpanist

- Play the rhythms below the line using the root of the chord, and the rhythms above the line using the fifth of the chord.
- Play rolls for long notes.
- Muffle where appropriate.
- Play and sing the rhythms at the same time.

➤ Snare Drum

- Play all the rhythms on the snare drum.
- Play the notes below the line with the left hand, and the notes above the line with the right hand.
- Play rolls for long notes.
- Set-up an isolated tom and play the notes above the line on the tom-tom, and the notes below the line on the snare, and visa versa.
- Use a mounted cowbell (with foot pedal) to play the downbeats, while playing the figures on the tom-tom and snare.

➤ Marimba, Xylophone, Bells or Vibraphone

- Play the notes below the line using the root of the chord, and the notes above the line using the fifth of the chord.
- Play rolls for long notes.
- Play and sing the rhythms at the same time.

Articulation Suggestions for Wind Instruments

Check with your teacher for additional articulation suggestions.

 Doo

 Dat

 Dot

 Ta

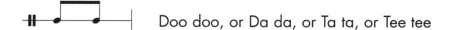 Doo doo, or Da da, or Ta ta, or Tee tee

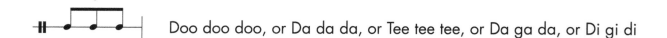 Doo doo doo, or Da da da, or Tee tee tee, or Da ga da, or Di gi di

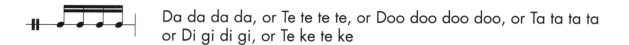 Da da da da, or Te te te te, or Doo doo doo doo, or Ta ta ta ta
or Di gi di gi, or Te ke te ke

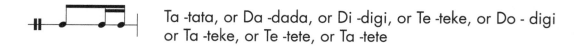 Ta -tata, or Da -dada, or Di -digi, or Te -teke, or Do - digi
or Ta -teke, or Te -tete, or Ta -tete

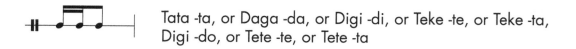 Tata -ta, or Daga -da, or Digi -di, or Teke -te, or Teke -ta,
Digi -do, or Tete -te, or Tete -ta

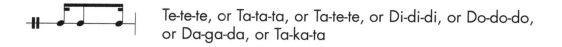 Te-te-te, or Ta-ta-ta, or Ta-te-te, or Di-di-di, or Do-do-do,
or Da-ga-da, or Ta-ka-ta

Articulation Suggestions for Vocalists

...ists can use the following suggested articulations for the exercises and studies in this book. Check with your
...or additional articulation suggestions.

...otes, the following articulations can be used.

 Ta, or De, or Te, or Doo, or Too, or Tay, or Kay, or Key, or Bee, or Shoo

 Ta, or Da, or Ba, or De, or Dee, or Bee

 Di gi, or Te ke, or Doo doo, or Da da, or Ta ta, or Tee tee or Da da,
or Cha cha, or Boo boo

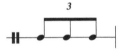 Doo doo doo, or Da da da, or Tee tee tee, or Da ga da, or Di gi di

 Te te te te, or Te-ke-te-ke, or De-ge-de-ge, or Too-koo-too-koo,
or Ta ta ta ta, or Sha-ga-sha-ga, or Boo-goo-boo-goo, or Be-de-be-de,
or Be-ge-be-ge, or Di gi gi gi, Da da da da, or Doo doo doo doo

 Da- digi, or Bah- dede, or Bop- digi, or Doo- digi, or doo- didi,
or Ta- teke, or Bah-bidi

 Doo-doo-baht, or Doo-doo-bop, or Za-ga-dat, or Be-de-baht,
or Boo-doo-bop, or Boo-doo-bee, or Di-gi-baht, or Di-gi-di

 Tata -ta, or Daga -da, or Digi -di, or Teke -te, or Teke -ta,
or Digi -do, or Tete -te, or Tete –ta

CD Styles and Track Listing

Track	Groove	Key	Notes to play	Tempo
1.	Big Band	B♭	B♭ & F	♩ = 110
2.	Caribbean Breeze	F	F & C	♩ = .10
3.	Cha-Cha	G	D & A	♩ = 130
4.	Disco Funk	G	G & D	♩ = 118
5.	Funk in Tres	E minor	E & B	♩ = 90
6.	Salsa	F	C & G	♩ = 102
7.	Funk R&B	G	D & A	♩ = 120
8.	Slow Groove	B♭	B♭ & F	♩ = 68
9.	Honey Samba	B♭	B♭ & F	♩ = 83
10.	Jazz Waltz	D minor	D & A	♩ = 110
11.	Merengue	C	C & G	♩ = 125
12.	Funk in Five	A	A & E	♩ = 90
13.	Gospel Groove	B♭	B♭ & F	♩ = 95
14.	Funk in Seven	A	A & E	♩ = 95
15.	Drum and Bass	D minor	D & A	♩ = 160
16.	Funky Hop	Any Key	Any Notes	♩ = 100
17.	Industrial	Any Key	Any Notes	♩ = 100